DOMINATING CONTROLLING FORCES

I do not understand what I do. For what I want to do I do not do, but what I hate I do.

Romans 7:15 *NIV*

by
Franklin N. Abazie

Dominating Controlling Forces
COPYRIGHT 2016 BY Franklin N Abazie
ISBN: 978-1-94513319-0

All right reserved. This book or any portion thereof may not be reproduced or used in any manner whatsoever without the express written permission of the publisher, except for the use of brief quotations in a book review. All Bible quotes are from King James Version and others as noted.

Published by: F N ABAZIE PUBLISHING HOUSE—
aka, Empowerment Bookstore

That I may publish with the voice of thanksgiving and tell of all thy wondrous works.
Psalm 26:7

To order additional copies, wholesales or booking call:
the Church office (973-372-7518)
or Empowerment Bookstore Hotline (973-393-8518)

Worship address:
343 Sanford Avenue, Newark, New Jersey 07106
Administrative Head Office address:
33 Schley Street Newark New Jersey 07112
Email: pastorfranknto@yahoo.com
Website www.fnabaziehealingministries.org
Publishing House: www.fnabaziepublishinghouse.org

This book is a production of F N Abazie Publishing House. A publication Arms of Miracle of God Ministries 2016.
First Edition

CONTENTS

THE MANDATE OF THE COMMISSION.....................iv
ARMS OF THE COMMISSION...................................v
INTRODUCTION...vi
CHAPTER 1
Overcoming the Lifestyle of Sin................................1
CHAPTER 2
Exposing the Weakness of the Devil........................8
CHAPTER 3
Overcoming the Spirit of Manipulation...................22
CHAPTER 4
Dominating Prevailing Forces Through Faith..........28
CHAPTER 5
Prayer of Salvation...47
About the Author...54

THE MANDATE OF THE COMMISSION

"The moment is due to impact your world through the revival of the healing & miracle ministry of Jesus Christ of Nazareth.

"I am sending you to restore health unto thee and I will heal thee of thy wounds, said the Lord of Host."

ARMS OF THE COMMISSION

1) F N Abazie Ministries—Miracle of God Ministries (Miracle Chapel Intl)

2) F N Abazie TV Ministries: Global Television Ministry Outreach

3) F N Abazie Radio Ministries: Radio Broadcasting Outreach

4) F N Abazie Publishing House: Book Publication

5) F N Abazie Bible School: also called Word of Healing Bible School (W.O.H.B.S.)

6) F N Abazie Evangelistic Ass: Miracle of God Ministries: Global Crusade

7) Empowerment Bookstore: Book distribution

8) F N Abazie Helping Hands: Meeting the Help of the Needy Worldwide

9) F N Abazie Disaster Recovery Mission: Global Disaster Recovery

10) F N Abazie Prison Ministry: Prison Ministry For All Convicts "Second Chance"

Some of our ministry arms are awaiting the appointed time to commence.

INTRODUCTION

For that which I do I allow not: for what I would, that do I not; but what I hate, that I do.
Romans 7:15

Without argument, there are forces in hell that have been delegated to buffet and manipulate the destinies of the Saints of God. Most clergys and a great number of laities in the body of Christ have neglected and ignored these forces of hell. If these forces remain at large, we the believer will suffer perpetual consequences at the judgment throne of God. It is my joy to share some deep secrets on how to contain and paralyze, strip him of all legal power and return him (Satan) to the perpetual chains of darkness where he belongs.

Most of us have lived in denial for almost all our lives. I tell you these forces are real and until you confront and destroy them, they will always have the upper hand to remote control your life and destiny. Even before you were born, God spoke concerning your life and destiny. But Satan has been torturing and manipulating your glorious destiny.

We, as the body of Christ, can no longer sit quietly while the people of God perish silently under these remote forces from hell. It is time to take the bull by the horn. One great man of God once said: "Every event is invented."

For the good that I would I do not: but the evil which I would not, that I do. Now if I do that I would not, it is no more I that do it, but sin that dwelleth in me.
Romans 7:19-20

You may not all agree with me, but I am persuaded to say this: Almost all of your life challenges have a spiritual root. All the hindrances, obstacles and attacks that have prevailed in your life are deeply rooted in the SPIRIT.

For we wrestle not against flesh and blood, but against principalities, against powers, against the rulers of the darkness of this world, against spiritual wickedness in high places.
Ephesians 6:12

In these last days, forces of evil have been let loose on a higher scale. These forces have power to intimidate, dominate and manipulate the lives and destinies of the believer. All witches cannot enforce the forces of evil without these three functions in place. In every stronghold there is a greater function of at least these three forces—Intimidate, Manipulate and Dominate.

In these last days the devil is at loose in numerous dimensions. Among the strongest tricks of the devil is to dominate, intimidate and manipulate the life and future of the believer. Nevertheless, there is an escape route for you. Among my reasons for writing is to arm you against all the wiles and schemes of the devil. We, the Saints of God, can no longer keep quiet while Satan snatches the lives of our love ones away.

Allow me to make this strong statement out of faith:

"SPIRITUAL battles are higher than PHYSICAL battles." With these lines in mind, until you overcome the enemy in the realms of the SPIRIT, the prevailing challenges has power to prevail. You will agree with me that at one point in your life experience, prevailing challenges have dominated and remote controlled your life involuntary. It is my desire in this book to expose and strip the devil naked of all his tricks and antics.

Believe me when I say these words: you are where you are today not because of your merit, nor physical might. Most of us steal God's GLORY and claim accolades and the due PRAISE that is due unto HIS NAME. Let me share these personal testimonies. Perhaps they will strengthen your faith. I know of a family friend and member who moved overseas in search of a better life. He was abroad doing well, making money and working hard to save his money. Suddenly, the devil came knocking at his heart. **"You must prepare now and visit Nigeria."**

This message prevailed and dominated his

thoughts and imagination until finally he succumbed to it. All of a sudden, we heard he was returning home. Without papers to return to his base, he arrived safely into Nigeria and, after a few months, began spending all his hard-earned money. Until one day he came to himself and began asking questions. (Why did I enter the airplane without a permanent residence paper to reside abroad before leaving my life overseas?)

Dominating controlling forces were against him and he was helpless to the challenge. In this book, the tricks and wiles of the devil are exposed and crushed. It is impossible for you to be dominated, manipulated and intimidated by Satan, as long as you read this book with understanding.

And there was in their synagogue a man with an unclean spirit and he cried out.
Mark 1:23

In these dreadful days we live in, unclean spirit is hovering in the air, seeking the next victim to launch an attack. The enemy has vowed to make men walk in all forms and appearance of uncleanliness. A young man who had plans for a great future finally got the capital he desired—and suddenly went on a shopping spree.

Despite all good advice from close family members, he ignored everybody's counsel and shopped to the last penny and became broke again. He only came to himself when he became broke and poor again. A greater trick of the devil is to his implementation of the Spirit of this world. Apostle Paul admonished us:

Now we have received, not the spirit of the world, but the spirit which is of God, that we might know the things that are freely given to us of God.
1 Corinthians 2:12

Without contradiction, the spirit of this world is a very destructive spirit. It will blind your eye with greed and a strong craving for material things. As long as you love the spirit of the world, it will not only draw you into craving material abundance, but it will increase your craving for acquiring money, leading you into a greedy lifestyle.

A great oil producing nation like Nigeria is a reflection of abject poverty because most of my countrymen and women are in bondage and in captivity to this spirit. *Beloved, I wish above all things that thou mayest prosper and be in health, even as thy soul prospereth.* (3 John 1:2) Most people misinterpret the above scripture. The prosperity of the soul is not on material things. The prosperity of the soul is a function of your contentment in life.

*Love not the world, neither the things that are
in the world. If any man love the world,
the love of the Father is not in him.
For all that is in the world, the lust of the flesh,
and the lust of the eyes, and the pride of life,
is not of the Father, but is of the world.
And the world passeth away, and the lust thereof:
but he that doeth the will of God abideth forever.*
1 John 2:15-17

From the above scripture, it's clear that the dominating controlling force is the acquisition of material worldly things. I read of a story recently where a known fraudster kingpin in Lagos pulled over his Range Rover SUV in the commotion of a crowded island and threw away his car keys before stripping himself naked.

Most good, moral people have gone the wrong way because these dominating forces have prevailed over their life. Jesus said to the Apostle Peter when he was manipulated in Mathew 16:23—*Get thee behind me, Satan: thou art an offense unto me: for thou savourest not the things that be of God, but those that be of men.*

Although the truth is bitter, most men and women of God who are not conscious of their spiritual walk with Jesus Christ have been manipulated, tortured, intimidated and dominated by these evil forces. It is my personal desire that the church of God expel these forces from our lives, family and ministry.

HAPPY READING!

HIGHLIGHTS

1) The depth of **FAITH** is a crucial weapon to evict the strong man (the devil).

2) **BOLDNESS** is a prevailing force that will drive all your oppositions far from you.

3) **THE POWER OF GOD** is sufficient to prevail against life challenges.

4) Without **AUTHORITY** you cannot prevail against life challenges.

5) **THE NAME OF JESUS IS THE POWER OF ATTORNEY** to obtain victory over dominating controlling forces.

6) The **last WEAPON to PULL the trigger** against the enemy is **THE BLOOD OF JESUS CHRIST**.

PRAYER POINT TO OVERCOME THE LIFESTYLE OF SIN

1) I destroy every manipulating thought of sin, in the Name of Jesus.

2) I crush every daily habit of sin in the Name of Jesus.

3) I cut from friendship leading me into sin, in the Name of Jesus.

4) Blood of Jesus, wash me afresh again, in the Name of Jesus.

5) Power of God, grant me the GRACE to live right for Jesus Christ.

6) Hand of God, deliver me from sin, in the Name of Jesus.

7) Fire of God, burn every sinful thought from my mind, in the Name of Jesus.

8) I proclaim authority over every prevailing sin in my life, in Jesus Name.

9) I destroy every root of sin in my life, in Jesus Name.

10) Sin shall not have dominion over my life, in the Name of Jesus.

11) Lord God, emphasize genuine repentance over my Spirit man, in the Name of Jesus

12) Holy Spirit, revive and rekindle your fire of revival inside of me, in the Name of Jesus.

13) Power of God, hijack the controlling forces oppressing my life, in the Name of Jesus.

14) Blood of Jesus, take over my life, in the Name of Jesus.

15) Lord God of heaven, open my mind to think right and do right, open my eyes to see right and open my ears to hear right, in the Name of Jesus.

Congratulations!

I thank God for your life. Now that you have repeated these prayers out loud, enjoy what the Holy Spirit is saying in this book.

GOD WILL GRANT YOU THE ADVANCED KNOWLEDGE TO OVERCOME ALL DOMINATING POWER CONTROLLING YOUR LIFE.

YOU WILL BECOME FREE IN DEED AS YOU READ THIS BOOK.

CHAPTER 1
OVERCOMING THE LIFESTYLE OF SIN

*For sin shall not have dominion over you:
for ye are not under the law, but under grace.*
Romans 6:14

For this evil generation of today, sin has become in vogue. The demand for sin and the requirement for immoralities has crumbled all the morally sound citizens. Man has left the biblical definition of marriage and has wandered into all forms and appearances of a lustful lifestyle. Although most of us will love to live a righteous lifestyle, the prevailing and dominating controlling forces of sin have forced almost everyone in this end time generation to accommodate the lifestyle of sin, at least to a degree.

A few days ago someone was telling me how they were "heartbroken" because they had recently broken out of a relationship. Without contradiction, I thought they were in a man/woman relationship. I was baffled and short of words when I discovered it was not the relationship I had in mind.

WHAT IS SIN, ONE MAY ASK?

One man said S.I.N means "Satan Identification Number. I do not disagree, but it is incomplete. In my own definition, sin is disobeying God's words and commandments. Every time you operate outside of the commandment of God, you are committing sin. *He that committeth sin is of the devil; for the devil sinneth from the beginning.* (1 John 3:8) For this purpose, the son of God was manifested that he might destroy the works of the devil.

Sin is a reproach to any nation.
Proverbs 14:34

Sin, as simple as it sounds, has the power to dominate anyone, even a whole nation. Sin is a virus that we all must fight against—especially its advancement into the body of Christ. *Be not overcome of evil, but overcome evil with good.* (Romans 12:21)

The evil bow before the good...
Proverbs 14:19

David proclaimed in Psalm 51:3—*For I acknowledge my transgressions and my sin is ever before me.* We must not take the purpose of the life and death of Jesus in vain. Although man by nature was born in sin like David attested, we are SPIRITS, WE HAVE A SOUL AND WE LIVE IN A BODY. *Behold I was shapen in iniquity; and in sin did my mother conceive me.* (Psalm 51:5)

Chapter 1 — Overcoming the Lifestyle of Sin

Knowing this, that our old man is crucified with him, that the body of sin might be destroyed, that henceforth we should not serve sin.
Romans 6:6

Although sin is a habit that, after a repeated circle, becomes a character. The lifestyle of sin is a remote control that remotes and HINDERS OUR DESTINY WITH CHRIST JESUS. Until you openly confess the Lord Jesus as your savior and repent of your sins, you remain a prey to the devil. *For with the heart, man believeth unto righteousness; and with the mouth confession is made unto salvation.* (Romans 10:10)

Then Peter said unto them, repent, and be baptized every one of you in the name of Jesus Christ for the remission of sins.
Acts 2:28

HOW DOES SIN DOMINATE & CONTROL OUR LIVES?

He that committeth sin is of the devil; for the devil sinneth from the beginning
1 John 3:8

Every time you are preoccupied with evil thoughts, evil ideas—any time you channel all your energy into negative thinking, negative imagination of evil and destruction, negative realization of bad things to affect and influence your environment—THAT is dominating, controlling forces in display. No man or preacher can change the way you process things, especially in your mind. Until you flush out all negative energy that is weighing on you, you are not ready for genuine deliverance. Until you embrace genuine salvation, you remain a mockery to the house of our God. As simple as salvation is, there is a price tag associated with it.

Now the works of the flesh are manifest, which are these; Adultery, fornication, uncleanness, lasciviousness, Idolatry, witchcraft, hatred, variance, emulations, wrath, strife, seditions, heresies, Envyings, murders, drunkenness, revellings, and such like: of the which I tell you before, as I have also told you in time past, that they which do such things shall not inherit the kingdom of God.
Galatians 5:19-21

In my opinion, any force designed to divert you from inheriting the kingdom of God is a dominating, controlling force. In the above scripture, it is attested—*Now the works of the flesh are manifest, which are these; Adultery, fornication, uncleanness, lasciviousness, Idolatry, witchcraft, hatred, variance, emulations, wrath, strife, seditions, heresies, Envyings, murders, drunkenness, revellings, and such like: of the which I tell you before, as I have also told you in time past, that they which do such things shall not inherit the kingdom of God.*

As long as you are living in sin, you are an agent of the devil and subject to his domination and control. For as much as you yield to sin, you are his tool and available for his use. *Know ye not, that to whom ye yield yourselves servants to obey, his servants ye are to whom ye obey; whether of sin unto death, or of obedience unto righteousness?* (Romans 6:16)

The scripture below is the summary of the resumé of the devil.

The thief cometh not, but for to steal, and to kill, and to destroy: I am come that they might have life, and that they might have it more abundantly.
John 10:10

Ye are of your father the devil, and the lusts of your father ye will do. He was a murderer from the beginning, and abode not in the truth, because there is no truth in him. When he speaketh a lie, he speaketh of his own: for he is a liar, and the father of it..
John 8:44

HOW DO I OVERCOME DOMINATING, CONTROLLING FORCES?

1) ***ACKNOWLEDGE*** you're a sinner. Christ died for your sins on the cross. (2 Corinthians 5:21, Romans 3:23)

2) ***REPENT:*** The greatest trick of the devil is not to lie to you. It is the assignment of the devil to make you interpret even scriptures in your own way. (Acts 3:19, Luke 13:5, 2 Peter 3:9) *Then Peter said unto them, Repent, and be baptized every one of you in the name of Jesus Christ for the remission of sins...* (Acts 2:38)

3) ***BELIEVE:*** For with the heart, man believeth unto righteousness...

4) ***CONFESS:*** Confess Jesus as the Lord over your life. *...and with the mouth confession is made unto salvation.* (Romans 10:10)

NOW SAY THIS PRAYER OUT LOUD:
"Say Lord Jesus, I accept you today as my Lord and my savior. Forgive me of my sins, wash me with your blood. Right now I believe I am sanctified, I am saved, I am free. I am free from the power of sin, to serve the Lord Jesus. Thank you, Lord, for saving me. Amen."

Congratulations.

YOU ARE NOW A BORN AGAIN CHRISTIAN!

Chapter 1   Overcoming the Lifestyle of Sin

HIGHLIGHTS OF CHAPTER ONE

1) All controlling forces domicile in sin.

2) The agenda of the devil is executed by domination, manipulation and intimidation.

3) The lifestyle of sin is the captivity of the devil.

4) The lifestyle of sin is a trap of the devil.

5) Conquer sin in your life and be free.

6) Until you yield to sin, you cannot be dominating, intimidated and remote controlled.

7) You are a blessing—not a curse.

CHAPTER 2
EXPOSING THE WEAKNESS OF THE DEVIL

*Be sober, be vigilant; because your adversary
the devil walks about like a roaring lion,
seeking whom he may devour.*
1 Peter 5:8

The devil is a weak devil. As long as you catch the revelation of the word of God, the devil cannot harrass you.

*Lest Satan should get an advantage of us:
for we are not ignorant of his devices.*
2 Corinthians 2:11

The devil has no other device but to decieve and to lie. All those funny dreams and nightmares are because of lack of the word of God in your heart. Catch the word of God and send the devil into the pit. The truth is; the devil has been defeated.

*Blotting out the handwriting of ordinances that
was against us, which was contrary to us,
and took it out of the way, nailing it to his cross;
And having spoiled principalities and powers, he made a
shew of them openly, triumphing over them in it.*
Colossians 2:14-15

Jesus Christ defeated the devil on the cross. As a believer, this truth must be evidenced in your life. We as believer are the spiritual law enforcement officers, with an accrediatation by the blood of Jesus. We are armed with the power, in the name of Jesus, which I call the power of the attorney for the arrest of all the schemes and wiles of the devil.

The thief cometh not, but for to steal, and to kill, and to destroy: I am come that they might have life, and that they might have it more abundantly.
John 10:10

The above scriptures say that the devil came to steal, to kill and to destroy. That is the entire resumé of the devil in a nutshell. But Jesus Christ came that we might have life and that we may have life in abundance.

WHAT ARE WE SAYING?

What we are saying here is that the devil is a weak devil who has been defeated by our lord Jesus Christ. The only way the devil can harrass us is if we give into his schemes and wiles. Fear is the only prominent weapon of the devil. I define fear as:

F---FALSE
E-----------EVIDENCE
A----------------------------APPEARING
R--REAL

For the thing which I greatly feared is come upon me,
and that which I was afraid of is come unto me.
Job 3:25

Fear is a snare, an opening that puts the enemy at an advantage. Every time we give in to fear we create an open door for the enemy to attack us. Job was very wealthy and normal until he began to be afraid of the enemy. **For the thing which I greatly feared is come upon me, and that which I was afraid of is come unto me.**

Neither give place to the devil.
Ephesians 4:27

To expose the weakness of the devil, we must stand strong in the faith. It is your faith in God that will put the enemy at bay (on the ground).

Wherefore take unto you the whole armour of God,
that ye may be able to withstand in the evil day,
and having done all, to stand. Stand therefore,
having your loins girt about with truth, and
having on the breastplate of righteousness.
Ephesians 6:13-14

The devil has no power over our lives. All the tricks and wiles of the devil have been subdued a very long time ago.

We must all put up a fight against the devil.

We must all contend with the adversary—the devil. The spiritual system is built in a dynamic fashion that no one can escape from—the confrontation and opposition of the enemy, the devil. Every Christian has Satan as his/her enemy to contend with.

Although unseen by the natural eye, this adversary is not imaginary nor a mythological character. Satan, the devil, is a person—a spirit being, with diabolic wisdom and a catastrophic intelligence. He has a mind and a will. He thinks, acts and reacts. Satan has the ability to manipulate even the most powerful man on earth today, if we let him. *Neither give place to the devil.* (Ephesians 4:27)

> *For we wrestle not against flesh and blood,*
> *but against principalities, against powers,*
> *against the rulers of the darkness of this world,*
> *against spiritual wickedness in high places.*
> **Ephesians 6:12**

For ages, most believers have suffered from the torture and torment of the devil. Almost every evil you can remember—from tribal wars to killing of any kind, murder, suicide, homicide, drug abuse, alcohol abuse— all were orchestrated by Satan and his cohorts. This unseen being is capable of destroying any man who permits him. Apostle Paul reminded us in Ephesians 4:27: *Neither give place to the devil.* This destroyer has tangible characteristics. He manipulates, intimidates and dominates ***"anyone who allows him."***

Remember, the sole incessant goal and ambition of the devil is to "steal, kill and destroy."

The thief cometh not, but for to steal, and to kill, and to destroy: I am come that they might have life, and that they might have it more abundantly.
John 10:10

24 hours every day, the enemy is on the prowl, seeking to cause mayhem and destruction to all believers and to contradict the work of Jesus Christ throughout the world. With military-like strategy and ruthless hostility, the devil aggressively searches for weakness in our faith and spiritual life, hoping to devour us with his lies, tricks, sin, deception, temptation or oppression—if we let him in. The Devil is the personification of all that is evil and is the author of every despicable end product of evil. We are reminded in Romans 12:21 to "***be not overcome of evil, but overcome evil with good.***"

Although we all have lived in ignorance of the truth, but whether you agree or live in continual denial, Satan has targeted you as a victim. He knows your name and address, your strengths and weaknesses. Somewhere in the shadows, he and his forces lurk, waiting, planning for the moment they will strike against you, especially when you are off-guard and not aware of an imminent attack.

*In whom the god of this world hath blinded
the minds of them which believe not,
lest the light of the glorious gospel of Christ,
who is the image of God, should shine unto them.*
2 Corinthians 4:4

A well-known strategy of the devil is to blind our mind from the truth. *Keep thy heart with all diligence; for out of it are the issues of life.* (Proverbs 4:23)

*I do not understand what I do. For what I want to do
I do not do, but what I hate I do.*
Romans 7:15 NIV

*Keep thy heart with all diligence;
for out of it are the issues of life.*
Proverbs 4:23

The above scripture carefully warns us to protect our mind from all appearance of evil thoughts, oppressive thoughts, hallucination, hearing strange voices, losing touch with the truth and the reality. Romans 12:2 tells us—***And be not conformed to this world: but be ye transformed by the renewing of your mind, that ye may prove what is that good, and acceptable, and perfect, will of God.***

Satan is desperate, hoping that you will, as many Christians do, remain ignorant of his reality so that you'll blame his assaults on somebody or something else. His method of operation is not straight forward He is "UNDERCOVER BLINDFOLDED." Subtly, he MANIPULATES hindering circumstances and inspires evil thoughts or temptations, disguising his activities behind the shroud of people or things. Satan will always seek to divert attention and blame for his actions upon others. But make no mistake, he is the real enemy, not your husband, wife, employer, government or Christian brethren. Satan INTIMIDATES the believer with the spirit of fear, traps us into his net with problems and challenges, hardship, difficulty, tribulations, court cases and trials—until that person submits to his imprisonment. Satan DOMINATES us by engaging our mind into the blame game. We tend to blame our mother-in-law, father-in-law, wife, husband, cousin, pastor or uncle. Most people are dominated simply by ignorance of the truth. Accepting the lies and tricks of the devil renders us all helpless.

For we do not wrestle against flesh and blood, but against principalities, against powers, against the rulers of the darkness of this age, against spiritual hosts of wickedness in the heavenly places.
Ephesians 6:12

SATAN HAS NO POWER OVER THE LIFE OF THE BELIEVER

Although the devil is described "like a roaring lion," in reality he has no actual power nor authority over believers. He seeks for your permission to exact and buffet on you, if you let him. He is not really a lion, but roars "like" a lion to bluff his victims into fear, intimidation, domination and manipulation. Satan is a liar and a deceiver. Satan uses tricks and deception as his weapon to gain advantage over those who are ignorant of the limitations of his power. *Lest Satan should get an advantage of us: for we are not ignorant of his devices.* (2 Corinthians 2:11)

Jesus Christ of Nazareth proved his divinity when he resurrected after three days from the grave. Satan has no power. Jesus triumphed over him on the cross and in the grave. Even in the grave, Jesus Christ is LORD.

When Jesus gave his life on the cross as the sacrifice for the sins of the world, He also redeemed us from Satan's power and dominion over us. *Having disarmed principalities and powers, He made a public spectacle of them, triumphing over them in it.* (Colossians. 2:15). *For this purpose the Son of God was manifested, that He might destroy the works of the devil.* (1 John 3:8) Satan is already a defeated devil. All his power is impotent as long as you acknowledge the Lord and become a born again believer. All of Satan's agenda and power were neutralized by the finished work of Christ on the cross.

EVERY BELIEVER HAS POWER & AUTHORITY OVER SATAN

Satan has no other strength than to deceive and trick us. He sells his blindfolded agenda through ignorance. Remember, he is a fallen angel who has been defeated on the cross. So if Satan is already defeated, why then is he still able to cause havoc? Because, even though Christ broke Satan's legal power, the Lord has left it up to us to "ENFORCE" the devil's defeated condition. We must all use the authority that Christ has given us to put Satan in his place.

As a believer, we need not fear Satan, but realize and exercise the authority which God has given you over the devil. Every person whose name has been recorded in the "Lamb's Book of Life" (all those who are saved) have been given authority over the power of the devil. *Behold, I give you the authority to trample on serpents and scorpions, and over all the power of the enemy, and nothing shall by any means hurt you.* (Luke 10:19) We all have right to exercise the authority of the name of Jesus to repel and drive Satan out of your territory and to break his grip over spiritual strongholds. (2 Corinthians 10:4) *When you recognize Satan's activity and covert operations, take authority over him in the name of Jesus! Just as Jesus and the early apostles did, command Satan to leave.* (Mark 16:17) The devil hates the name of Jesus and detests an atmosphere of praise and worship which exalts the name of Jesus. Christ said, *"For where two or three are gathered together in my name, I am there in the midst of them."* (Matthew 18:20) Be assured, the presence of Christ will expel the presence of Satan. Build your faith by the help of the Holy Spirit. Exercise dominion and a lifestyle of joy as it sends the devil packing to his pits where he belongs.

GIVE NO PLACE TO THE DEVIL

Remember, the name of Jesus DESTROYS Satan. But it would be no benefit to evict Satan and his agents, when we encourage an open door for him to enter into our lives, to manipulate us. The Bible tells us to not "give place" for the devil. (Ephesians 4:27) That is, provide no area of your life where Satan can be comfortable or establish strongholds. The enemy can always be found working in those who entertain sin, disobedience, rebellion or a self-willed nature.

Unforgiveness toward others is another area which Satan flourishes. (2 Corinthians 2:11) Furthermore, any area of your life which is not submitted to God is considered open territory to the devil, and he has the right to bring his expanding influence to those areas. This is why the scripture says, *"...submit to God. Resist the devil and he will flee from you."* (James 4:7)

The only way to actually resist Satan is to submit yourself fully to God. This was what Jesus was referring to when He said, *"...the ruler of this world is coming, and he has nothing in me."* (John 14:30) Jesus had submitted himself to God, and although the devil would try Him, there was nothing for the devil to use to gain an advantage. God is in you, and YOU have been given power over the devil! By submitting to God, and exercising your authority in the name of Jesus, you are more powerful than the enemy. *"...He who is in you is greater than he who is in the world."* (1 John 4:4)

Lest Satan should get an advantage of us: for we are not ignorant of his devices.
2 Corinthians 2:11

CONCLUSION

The strength of the devil is hidden in sin and doing the wrong thing in life. Once you come out of sin, Satan has no power to dominate nor manipulate your life. The light of the word of God is the information that creates awareness of the devil devices. The devil uses ignorance to blind our mind from the truth of the word of God. As long as you uphold the standard of the Bible, the devil will stay far from oppressing your life.

In our lifetime, we must make critical decisions that affect our future. Therefore, pray and ask God to open your eyes to all the devices the enemy is using against you in Jesus Name.

PRAYER POINT TO ACTIVATE THE PRESENCE OF THE HOLY SPIRIT

1) Holy Spirit, reveal yourself to me, in the Name of Jesus.

2) Holy Spirit, crush every daily habit of sin, in the Name of Jesus.

3) Holy Spirit, become my companion today, in the Name of Jesus.

4) Holy Spirit, grant me access, in the Name of Jesus.

5) Power of God, grant me the GRACE to live right for Jesus Christ.

6) Hand of God, deliver me from sin, in the Name of Jesus.

7) Fire of God, burn every sinful thoughts from my mind, in the Name of Jesus.

8) I proclaim authority over every prevailing sin in my life, in Jesus Name.

9) I destroy every root of sin in my life, in Jesus Name.

10) Sin shall not have dominion over my life, in the Name of Jesus.

11) Lord God, emphasize genuine repentance over my spirit man, in the Name of Jesus

12) Holy Spirit, revive and rekindle your fire of revival inside of me, in the Name of Jesus.

13) Power of God, hijack the controlling forces oppressing my life, in the Name of Jesus.

14) Blood of Jesus, take over my life, in the Name of Jesus.

15) O Lord, baptize me with the gift of the Holy Spirit.

16) Holy Spirit, breathe afresh upon my life, in the Name of Jesus.

17) Holy Spirit, take possession of my will, in the Name of Jesus.

18) Holy Spirit, make yourself real to me, in the name of Jesus.

19) Holy Spirit, fan your revival fire upon my life, in the name of Jesus.

20) The devil must remain weak and paralyzed over my life, in the Name of Jesus.

HIGHLIGHTS OF CHAPTER TWO

1) The devil is a weak devil with no power.

2) The devil fears the word of God.

3) What you allow has power to remain.

4) What you resist cannot remain.

5) Revelation of the word of God is the eviction of the devil.

6) What you confront, you must conquer.

Catch the word of God and catch your vision from God.

CHAPTER 3
OVERCOMING
THE SPIRIT OF MANIPULATION

*I do not understand what I do. For what I want to do
I do not do, but what I hate I do.*
ROMANS 7:15 *NIV*

The American heritage dictionary defines the word manipulation as follows: *To operate or control by skilled use of the hands; to influence or manage shrewdly or deviously; to tamper with or falsify for personal gain.* In my view all these definitions are just another interpretation of the work of evil forces. The devil exploits, tries to maneuver our finances, marriage, education and to reshape our destiny. The sole aim of Satan is to influence, manage or to establish control and authority over our lives by indirect mean. *For the good that I would I do not: but the evil which I would not, that I do.* (Romans 7:19)

The spirit of manipulation because it is hidden in SIN, is spreading like wide fire all over the globe. As a child of God there certain stronghold forces we must be cautious in life. Briefly let's examine all such avenues that the devil is using to influence and manipulate our lives in this end time.

THE SPIRIT OF THE WORLD

Now we have received, not the spirit of the world, but the spirit which is of God; that we might know the things that are freely given to us of God.
1 Corinthians 2:12

This is very simple. If you can avoid being influenced by what you see these days on television, in stores and in the movies, you will be free as a believer. The SPIRIT OF THIS WORLD attracts and influences our lives into craving after some worldly things that have no value nor brings GLORY TO HIS NAME. We were warned in this passage:

Love not the world, neither the things that are in the world. If any man love the world, the love of the Father is not in him. For all that is in the world, the lust of the flesh, and the lust of the eyes, and the pride of life, is not of the Father, but is of the world. And the world passeth away, and the lust thereof: but he that doeth the will of God abideth for ever..
1 John 2:15-17

The spirit of this world supervises and influences our lives to crave after lustful things. It makes us buy things, even on credit cards, knowing we cannot repay—and we blame the devil. It makes us show pride when it is not necessary. (It was pride that killed these men in the Bible—Pharaoh, Nebuchadnezzar, Herod).

Have you forgotten this scripture? *The meek will he guide in judgment: and the meek will he teach his way.* (Psalm 25:9)

Moses was the meekest man on earth and he became the great.

Now the man Moses was very meek, above all the men which were upon the face of the earth.
Numbers 12:3

And there arose not a prophet since in Israel like unto Moses, whom the Lord knew face to face.
Deuteronomy 34:10

Remember…

Humble yourselves therefore under the mighty hand of God, that he may exalt you in due time.
1 Peter 5:6

Jesus Christ made it clear to us:

These things I have spoken unto you, that in me ye might have peace. In the world ye shall have tribulation: but be of good cheer; I have overcome the world.
John 16:33

In your lifetime, you will be confronted by certain obstacles and hindrances. But be encouraged in the faith that with GOD you CAN do all things. As a believer, do not allow the spirit of manipulation to intimidate nor influence your lifestyle. The fact that you are struggling with your finances doesn't mean you should go steal from anybody. The fact that things are not moving as you desire does not mean you should be depressed and go into drinking alcohol and smoking drugs. That you suffered a disaster or bitter divorce does not mean you should commit suicide.

The Bible says in Ecclesiastes 9:4—*For to him that is joined to all the living there is hope: for a living dog is better than a dead lion.*

LYING SPIRITS

And the Lord said unto him, Wherewith? And he said, I will go forth, and I will be a lying spirit in the mouth of all his prophets. And he said, Thou shalt persuade him, and prevail also: go forth, and do so.
1 Kings 22:22

Demonic agents enforce the spirit of manipulation through lying spirits. Oftentimes people lie—even to themselves. If you can truly open your eyes, there is something great inside of you. Lying spirit manipulates men and women in marriage into cheating, hate, resentment, malice, bitterness, anger, envy and divorce.

Lying spirit is an agent of manipulation. I admonish you to stop all lying forces remoting your life, in the Name of Jesus.

SPIRIT OF WHOREDOMS

They will not frame their doings to turn unto their God: for the spirit of whoredoms is in the midst of them, and they have not known the Lord.
Hosea 5:4

The severity of the spirit of whoredoms is that it is a combination of three or more forces of the world. It is a combination of the lust of the flesh, the lust of the eyes and the pride of life. This is the spirit that leads men and women into all sort sof unquenchable immoral sexual appetites. The forces of whoredoms are very strong to break, because they develop early in a young adult. These are the forces responsible for infidelity in marriage and responsible for the high rate of divorce we see today.

And even as they did not like to retain God in their knowledge, God gave them over to a reprobate mind, to do those things which are not convenient...
Romans 1:28

Manipulation is a device of the enemy to buffet you.

REVIEW OF CHAPTER THREE

1) Never allow circumstances to manipulate your life.

2) Never give room for the devil.

3) Always stand in faith.

4) Never give up in life.

5) Winner do not quit.

6) Believers do not quit.

7) Never be afraid for any reason in life.

8) Always be conscious of the hand of God in your life.

9) Always rebuke the devil from your life challenges.

Here are scriptures to remember in challenging times:

And Jesus answering saith unto them,
Have faith in God.
Mark 11:22

As soon as Jesus heard the word that was spoken,
he saith unto the ruler of the synagogue,
Be not afraid, only believe.
Mark 5:36

CHAPTER 4
DOMINATING PREVAILING FORCES THROUGH FAITH

Quenched the violence of fire, escaped the edge of the sword, out of weakness were made strong, waxed valiant in fight, turned to flight the armies of the aliens.
Hebrews 11:34

In my own definition, any force that has power to stop you from going forward in any defined destination or attainment in life is a prevailing force. For example, you have an education—but you have not been hired by any corporation and you've had to settle for becoming a TAXI DRIVER. Or if you are in school and you've settled for a lower degree—say from ENIGINEERING into BUSINESS MANAGEMENT. Or instead of buying your own house, you've settled for renting. All of these forces are hindering forces that produce frustration, anger and depression. *Hope deferred maketh the heart sick: but when the desire cometh, it is a tree of life.* (Proverbs 13:12)

Without faith, these hindering forces that will stop you from fulfilling your GOD ORDAINED DESTINY in life. If you double check with me, how many times have you settled for an alternative choice in your life? Perhaps because you're short on finances (MON-

EY) and you've settled for a cheaper car or you settled for a cheaper version of your original plan. The result of these prevailing forces are frustration, anger, envy, depression.

For ages, faith has played a major role in shaping lives and destinies. In my own small definition, FAITH means EXPECTING a good outcome from a negative circumstance—while FEAR means EXPECTING a bad outcome out of a POSITIVE situation. GOD works with your FAITH, while Satan works with your FEAR. Most of us claim, we have faith—but we lack action. *For as the body without the spirit is dead, so faith without works is dead also.* (James 2:26)

Although the POWER OF FAITH is the primary shield to overcome prevailing dominating forces, evil prevailing forces cannot be subdued without the forces of DECISION and WILL POWER alone.

FAITH MUST COME INTO PLAY.

Both in the natural sense and in the realms of the SPIRIT, the POWER OF DECISION & WILLPOWER is the stronghold to overcome dominating prevailing forces. Jesus made it clear. *These things I have spoken unto you, that in me ye might have peace. In the world ye shall have tribulation: but be of good cheer; I have overcome the world.* (John 16:33)

In my opinion, as long as you are conscious of the wiles and schemes of the devil, Satan and his cohorts will forever distant themselves from you. Jesus said in this world *"ye shall have tribulation, but be of good cheer"*—we are all destined to overcome the wicked one.

There hath no temptation taken you but such as is common to man: but God is faithful, who will not suffer you to be tempted above that ye are able; but will with the temptation also make a way to escape, that ye may be able to bear it.
1 Corrinthians 10:13

Temptation, in my own interpretation, means a test of your faith. Apostle Peter was tested three times and he failed them all. Every time temptation or trouble comes into your life, take it that you are on a test from GOD. *Talk no more so exceeding proudly; let not arrogancy come out of your mouth: for the Lord is a God of knowledge, and by him actions are weighed.* (1 Samuel 2:3)

You cannot dominate prevailing forces without dealing with the root cause of those forces. I call the root cause REMOTE CONTROL FORCES.

SUBDUING REMOTE CONTROL FORCES

Who through faith subdued kingdoms, wrought righteousness, obtained promises, stopped the mouths of lions.
Hebrews 11:3

And God blessed them, and God said unto them,
Be fruitful, and multiply, and replenish the earth,
and subdue it: and have dominion over
the fish of the sea, and over the fowl of the air,
and over every living thing that moveth upon the earth..
Genesis 1:28

Let us hear the conclusion of the whole matter:
Fear God, and keep his commandments:
for this is the whole duty of man.
For God shall bring every work into judgment,
with every secret thing, whether it be good,
or whether it be evil.
Ecclesiastes 12:13-14

Most remote control forces appear in our dreams through diverting images. Anything you are worried about and afraid of is usually what the devil uses to harass and torture you. **Let's briefly examine a few remote control forces:**

FEAR—

F......False

E............Evidence

A........................Appearing

R....................................Real

For the thing which I greatly feared is come upon me,
and that which I was afraid of is come unto me.
Job 3:25

Developing a faith-winning mentality is the only way to overcome all the trials and obstacles and challenges of life. Your mentality about your life and your vision for your future is the only way you can dominate all the obstacles of life—financial challenges, relationship struggles, etc.

Nay, in all these things we are more than conquerors
through him that loved us. For I am persuaded,
that neither death, nor life, nor angels,
nor principalities, nor powers, nor things present,
nor things to come, Nor height, nor depth,
nor any other creature, shall be able to
separate us from the love of God,
which is in Christ Jesus our Lord.
Romans 8:37-39

PRAYER POINTS TO DOMINATE REMOTE CONTROL FORCES

1) Father Lord, deliver me from marine forces, in the Name of Jesus.

2) Fire of God, open my spiritual eyes to see and hear from you.

3) Lamb of God, favor me, in Jesus Name.

4) I bled the blood of Jesus Christ over my life.

5) Holy Spirit, reveal your plans over my life, in the Name of Jesus.

6) Finger of God, deliver me from frustrating forces waging against my life and destiny.

7) I dominate all family spells, in the Name of Jesus.

8) Holy Ghost, fire roast every familiar strongman in my life.

CONCLUSION

Examine yourselves, whether ye be in the faith;
prove your own selves. Know ye not your own selves,
how that Jesus Christ is in you, except ye be reprobates?
2 Corinthians 13:5

It is time to examine yourselves; we cannot continue to lie to ourselves. It is time to tell your self the TRUTH.

What have you attempted and it never worked out for you in your life?

What could have been done more to
my vineyard that I have not done in it?
Isaiah 5:4

Winners never quit in this race of life, regardless of the prevailing challenges as you examine yourself. Build up a menatlity never to quit. As long as you live, you must strive for a higher mark.

Brethren, I count not myself to have apprehended:
but this one thing I do, forgetting those things
which are behind, and reaching forth
unto those things which are before,
I press toward the mark for the prize
of the high calling of God in Christ Jesus.
Philippians 3:13-14

We must all continue in our pursuit of happiness, excellence in life and eternal life without fear.

Henry Ford said: "Failure is simply the opportunity to begin again, this time more intelligently."

FAIL means:

F……..First

A……………..Attempt

I………………………….In

L……………………………………..Learning

If you are depressed, you are living in the past.

If you are anxious, you are living in the future.

If you are at peace, you are living in the present.

Do NOT give up on your dreams. God will not give up fulfiling it for you in life.

Wherefore take unto you the whole armour of God that ye may be able to withstand in the evil day, and having done all, to stand.
Ephesians 6:14

As long as you BELIEVE IN GOD and HAVE FAITH IN GOD, those forces oppressing you must be subdued. Jesus Christ paid the ultimate price—therefore you must claim liberty and freedom in Jesus Christ as you read this book.

DECISION KEYS

1) Nothing changes until you make up your mind.

2) Decision is the gateway to deliverance.

3) Until you decide, no one will decide for you.

4) Your prosperity is proportional to your decisions.

5) The decision you make will determine the future you will create

6) Decision creates future and fulfills destinies.

7) Decision beautifies our future.

8) Decision keeps you out of trouble.

9) Decision exempts you from evil.

10) Decision gurantees eternity.

11) You can only go far in life by your faith decisions.

12) You are poor because you made such decisions

13) Make a decision and change your life.

14) Life changing decisions are a function of quality information.

15) Success in life is a function of decision.

16) Life experiences are full of decisions.

17) Decisions change destinies.

18) Never settle for information—always look for revelation.

19) You are where you are today based on your last decision.

20) Information is crucial in decision making.

21) Decision makers rule the world.

22) You can rule your world with quality decisions.

23) As long as you decide rightly, Satan cannot harrass you.

WISDOM KEYS

— Every productive society is a society heading to the top.

— Millions of Nigerians run away from Nigeria. Very few Nigerians stay in Nigeria.

— My decision to return Nigeria is the will of God for my life.

— My shortcoming in America after 18 years is the fact that I've trained me to be wise, to think, reflect and reason appropriately.

— If you train your mind to reason, it will train your hands to earn money.

— It is absurd to use the money of the heathen to build the kingdom of the living God.

— Every ministry reveals its agenda and VISION either at the beginning or at the end.

— Be careful of your life. It is your first ministry.

— The average American mind is conditioned for a continual quest to get new things and discard the old.

—When I considered well, my BMW jeep became my initial deposit for the work of the ministry in Nigeria.

—Money will never fall from any tree or person. Make up your mind to be independent today.

—Everyone is waiting for you to change your mind. Until you change your thinking, nothing changes around you.

—Multiple academic degrees in other disciplines gave me the chance to think and reason.

—Whatever anyone is thinking at any time reveals what is inside of their heart.

—All planned events are the product of meditation.

—Every event is designed for a designated timeline.

—Wisdom is your ability to think, to create and invent.

— If you can think wisely enough, you will come out of debt.

—The distance between you and your success is your innovative and creative ability to think well.

—Success is the result of hard work, commitment, resolve and determined learning from past mistakes and failings.

—If you organize your mind, you have organized your life and destiny.

—There is a thin line between success and failure.

—Wealth is your ability to think, power is your ability to reason and success is your ability to be informed.

—If you can make use of your mind by thinking and reasoning, God will make use of your life and destiny.

—Reflect, reason, think and be Great.

—Famous people are born of woman.

—That you will make it is your intention, that you will survive is your resolve, that you will succeed with changes is your determination, personal efforts and hard work.

—No man was born a failure.

—Lack of vision is the result of failure.

—Working with mental patients encourages and aspire me to be a productive observant and dedicated to my assignment.

—Successful people are not magicians. It is the will-power, combined with hard work and determination and a resolve to succeed, that make them succeed.

—In the unequivocal state of the mind, intention is not a location or a position. It is the state of the mind.

—So many people think that they think.

—The mind is used to think, to reflect and to reason.

—You will remain blind with your eyes open until you can see with your mind by thinking.

—There is no favoritism in accurate and precise calculation.

—Although knowledge is power, information is the key and gateway to a great future.

—It will take the hand of God to move the hand of man.

—With the backing of the great wise God, nothing will disconnect you from your inheritance.

—As long as you have wisdom and understanding of God, Satan and evil cannot manipulate your life and destiny.

—You have come this far in life by your own judgment and the decisions you made in the past. Now lean in and listen to God for another dimension of greatness.

—Great people are ordinary people. It is extra ordinary efforts and the price of sacrifice that produces greatness in them.

—As a mental direct care worker, I saw a great pastor and a motivational speaker within myself.

—A menial job does not reduce your self-worth. Until you resolve to achieve greatness and see greatness in all you do, you will never count in your community.

—The principle of Jesus will solve your gambling and addiction problems.

—The man of Jesus will lead you into heaven.

—Everyone has their self-appraisal and what they think about you. Until you discover yourself, other opinions about you will alter the real you.

—Supervisors and directors are just a position in the chain of command in a workplace. Never allow your supervisor hierarchy to alter your opinion of yourself.

—Everyone can come out of debt if they make up their mind.

—The fact that I am not a decision-maker at work does not diminish my contribution to my world.

—Although it appears like it was a poor decision to accept a direct care employment at a psychiatric hospital, as I reflect on my nine years of that experience, it became apparent that I have learned and experienced enough for my next assignment.

—Self-encouragement and determination is a resolve of the heart.

—If you are determined to make a difference and do the things that make a difference, you will eventually make a difference.

—Good things do not come easy.

—Short cuts will cut your life short.

—Those who look ahead move ahead.

—Life is all about making an impact. In your lifetime strive to make an impact in your community.

—Make friends and connect with people who are moving ahead of you in life.

—If you can look around well, you have come a long way in your life, made a lot of difference and realized a lot of success in life.

—If you are my old friend, hurry up to reach out to me before I become a stranger to you.

—I am blessed with inspirations from God that changed my interpretation of the world around me.

—I thought I was stagnant and lonely until I looked around and noticed my children running around and my wife cooking.

— At 40, I resigned my job to seek the Lord forever.

—My ministry took a drastic rise to the top when the wisdom of God visited me with knowledge and understanding.

—You will be a better person if you understand the characteristics of your personality like your mood swings, attitudes and habits.

—It is the seed of love you sow into the heart of a child and a woman that you reap in due time.

—Love is not selfish. Love shares everything, including the concealed secrets of the mind.

—As long as you have a prayer life and a Bible, you will never feel lonely in the race of life.

—When good friends disconnect from you, let them go. They might have seen something new in a different direction.

—Confidence in yourself and in God is the only way to bring you out of captivity

—Never train a child to waste his or her time.

—The mind is the greatest asset of a great future.

—You walk by common sense, run by principles and fly by instruction.

—Those who become successful in life did it by self-determination, hard work and learning from past failures.

—Most successful people are lonely people. No one renders help to them, believing they are already successful. Except when they seek for more knowledge and information, they are all alone.

— I have seen a towing truck vehicle. I have also seen a towing ship in the water. But I have never seen a towing airplane in the air.

—I exercise my judgment and make a decision every minute of the day. Decisions are crucial, critical and vital with reference to your future.

—So many people wish for a great future. You can only work towards a great future.

—Your celebrity status began when you discovered your talent. What are you good at? Work at it with all your commitment.

—Prayers will sustain you, but the wisdom of God will prosper you.

—When I met Oyedepo, his teachings changed my perspective. But when I met Ibiyeomie, his teaching changed my perception.

— It took the late Dr. Norman Vincent Peale's book to open my mind towards the kingdom of success.

CHAPTER 5
PRAYER OF SALVATION

WHAT IS SALVATION?

Salvation means deliverance from your sins and sickness and redemption of your soul. There is no other way we all can be saved except by the Name of Jesus Christ of Nazareth.

Neither is there salvation in any other:
for there is none other name under heaven
given among men, whereby we must be saved.
Acts 4:12

I am glad you have read this book all the way from the beginning to this point. All I have said from the beginning will remain a mystery until you commit it into practice.

If you have not given your life to Jesus, do so now. Give your life to Christ. Know the truth today for yourself! The truth is that Jesus died for your sins. And because He died, you must be alive and prosperous.

What must I do to determine my divine visitation?

To determine divine visitation you must be born again! The word says as many as received Him, to them gave He power to become the sons of God.

Even to them that believe on His name.

To qualify for divine visitation, do the following sincerely:

1) Acknowledge that you are a sinner and that He died for you. (Romans 3:23)

2) Repent of your sins. (Acts 3:19, Luke 13:5, 2 Peter 3:9)

3) Believe in your heart that Jesus died for your sin. (Romans 10:10)

4) Confess Jesus as the Lord over your life. (Romans 10:10, Acts 2:21)

NOW REPEAT THIS PRAYER ALOUD:
Say Lord Jesus, I accept you today, as my Lord and my savior, forgive me of my sins wash me with your blood. Right now, I believe, I am sanctified, I am save, I am free, I am free from the Power of sin to serve the Lord Jesus. Thank you Lord for saving me. Amen.

Congratulations.

YOU ARE NOW A BORN AGAIN CHRISTIAN!

Again, I say to you—congratulations! I adjure you to watch the Spirit of God bear witness with your

Spirit confirming His word with signs following. The word says the Spirit itself beareth witness with our spirit, that we are the children of God.

MY HEARTFELT PRAYER FOR YOU

It is my burning desire for God to touch you through one of our teaching books or CDs. It also my personal desire for you encounter God for yourself.

Now let me pray for you:

O Lord God! I beseech thee, and through personal prayer intercession today that the Holy Spirit will touch the precious soul reading this book and turn their life around. Spirit of God, possess this loved one. Lord, overcome all dominating, controlling forces that have prevailed over their lives. I come against all oppressive thought, in Jesus Name. Henceforth, I pronounce you free from manipulation, intimidation and domination of the wicked enemy called the devil. You are free from all satanic harassment and assaults. Amen.

MIRACLE CARE OUTREACH

*"...But that the members should have
the same care one for another"*
1 Corinthians 12:25

We are all members of the body of Christ. Jesus commanded us to love our neighbor as ourselves. This includes caring for one another as a member of one body. True love is expressed in caring and giving. The word says, for God so Love He gave....

Reach out to someone in need of Jesus. Help someone in crisis find Christ. Look out and prove your love to Jesus by caring and inviting your friends and associates to find Jesus the Healer.

Invite your friends to our Home Care Cell Fellowship (Miracle Chapel Intl. Satellite Fellowship). We're in the U.S. at 33 Schley Street, Newark, New Jersey 07112. Home Care Cell Fellowship Group meets every Tuesday at 6:00pm-7:00pm.

If you are in Nigeria—MIRACLE OF GOD MINISTRIES, aka "MIRACLE CHAPEL INTL." Mpama–Egbu-Owerri Imo state Nigeria.

LIFE IS NOT ALL ABOUT DURATION, BUT IT'S ALL ABOUT DONATION

What does this statement mean?

Life consists not in accumulation of material wealth. (Luke 12:15) But it's all about liberality...i.e., what you can give and share with others. (Proverbs 11:25) When you live for others, you live forever—because you outlive your generation by the legacy you leave behind after you depart into glory to be with the Lord. But when you live for yourself, when you are reduced to SELF—you are easily forgotten when you die and depart in glory.

Permit me to admonish you today to live your life to be a blessing to a soul connected to you today. I want you to know that so many souls are connected and looking up to you, and through you so many souls will be saved and rescued from destruction. Will you disciple someone today to find Jesus Christ?

As a genuine Christian, it is your duty to evangelize Jesus Christ to all you meet on your way. Jesus is still in the healing business—Jesus is still doing miracles, from time of old to now. Therefore, tell someone about Jesus Christ today, disciple and bring them to Church. *Philip findeth Nathanael...* (John 1:45)

Please prove the sincerity of your love for God today, please become a soul winner. The dignity of your Christianity is hidden in your boldness to proclaim and evangelize Jesus Christ to all you meet on your way. There is a question mark on the integrity of your Christianity until you become a life soul winner. Invite someone to join us worship the Lord Jesus this coming Sunday.

MIRACLE OF GOD MINISTRIES
PILLARS OF THE COMMISSION

We Believe, Preach and Practice the following:

1) We believe and preach Salvation to every living human being.

2) We believe and preach Repentance and Forgiveness of sins.

3) We believe and preach the baptism of the Holy Spirit and Spiritual gifts.

4) We believe and teach Prosperity.

5) We believe and preach Divine Healing and Miracles—Signs and Wonder.

6) We believe and preach Faith.

7) We believe and proclaim the Power of God (Supernatural).

8) We believe and proclaim Praise and Worship to God.

9) We believe and preach Wisdom.

10) We believe and preach Holiness (Consecration).

11) We believe and preach Vision.

12) We believe and teach the Word of God.

13) We believe and teach Success.

14) We believe and practice Prayer.

15) We believe and teach Deliverance.

These 15 stones form the Pillars of Our Commission.

ABOUT THE AUTHOR

Rev. Franklin N. Abazie is the founding and Presiding Pastor of Miracle of God Ministries, with headquarters in Newark, New Jersey USA and a branch church in Owerri-Imo State Nigeria. He is following the footsteps of one of his mentors, the healing evangelist Oral Roberts of the blessed memory. The Lord passed Oral Roberts' healing mantle two days before he went to be with the Lord at age 91 into the hands of healing evangelist Rev. Franklin N. Abazie in a vision.

In all his services, the Power and Presence of God is present to heal all in his audience. Rev. Abazie is an ordained man of God, with a Healing Ministry reviving the healing and miracle ministry of Jesus

Christ of Nazareth.

Pastor Franklin N. Abazie, has been called by God with a unique mandate: **"THE MOMENT IS DUE TO IMPACT YOUR WORLD THROUGH THE REVIVAL OF THE HEALING AND MIRACLE MINISTRY OF JESUS CHRIST OF NAZARETH.**

"I AM SENDING YOU TO RESTORE HEALTH UNTO THEE AND I WILL HEAL THEE OF THY WOUNDS, SAID THE LORD OF HOST"

Rev. Abazie is a gifted, ardent teacher of the word of God, who operates also in the office of a Prophet, generating and attracting undeniable signs and wonders, special miracles and healings, with apostolic fireworks of the Holy Ghost. He is the founding and presiding senior Pastor of this fast growing Healing Ministry. He has written over 86 inspirational, healing and transforming books covering almost all aspects of divine healing and life. He is happily married and blessed with children.

BOOKS BY REV. FRANKLIN N. ABAZIE:

1) The Outcome of Faith
2) Understanding the Secret of Prevailing Prayers
3) Commanding Abundance
4) Understanding the Secret of the Man God Uses
5) Activating My Due Season
6) Overcoming Divine Verdicts
7) The Outcome of Divine Wisdom
8) Understanding God's Restoration Mandate
9) Walking In the Victory and Authority of the Truth
10) God's Covenant Exemption
11) Destiny Restoration Pillars
12) Provoking Acceptable Praise
13) Understanding Divine Judgment
14) Activating Angelic Re-enforcement
15) Provoking Un-Merited Favo
16) The Benefits of the Speaking Faith
17) Understanding Divine Arrangement
18) How to Keep Your Healing
19) Understanding the Mysteries of the Speaking Faith
20) Understanding the Mysteries of Prophetic Healing
21) Operating Under the Rules of Creative Healing
22) Understanding the Joy of Breakthrough
23) Understanding the Mystery of Breakthrough
24) Understanding Divine Prosperity
25) Understanding Divine Healing
26) Retaining Your Inheritance
27) Overcoming Confusing Spirit
28) Commanding Angelic Escorts

29) Enforcing Your Inheritance In Christ Jesus
30) Understanding Your Guardian Angels
31) Overcoming the Dominion of Sin
32) Understanding the Voice of God
33) The Outstanding Benefits of the Anointing
34) The Audacity of the Blood of Jesus
35) Walking in the Reality of the Anointing
36) Escaping the Nightmare of Poverty
37) Understanding Your Harvest Season
38) Activating Your Success Buttons
39) Overcoming the Forces of Darkness
40) Overcoming the Devices of the Devil
41) Overcoming Demonic Agents
42) Overcoming the Sorrows of Failure
43) Rejecting the Sorrows of Failure
44) Resisting the Sorrows of Poverty
45) Restoring Broken Marriages
46) Redeeming Your Days
47) The Force of Vision
48) Overcoming the Forces of Ignorance
49) Understanding the Sacrifice of Small Beginning
50) The Might of Small Beginning
51) Understanding the Mysteries of Prophesy
52) Overcoming Dream Nightmares
53) Breaking the Shackles of the Curse of the Law
54) Understanding the Joy of Harvest
55) Wisdom for Signs & Wonders
56) Wisdom for Generational Impact
57) Wisdom for Marriage Stability
58) Understanding the Number of Your Days

59) *Enforcing Your Kingdom Rights*
60) *Escaping the Traps of Immoralities*
61) *Escaping the Trap of Poverty*
62) *Accessing Biblical Prosperity*
63) *Accessing True Riches in Christ*
64) *Silencing the Voice of the Accuser*
65) *Overcoming the Forces of Oppositions*
66) *Quenching the Voice of the Avenger*
67) *Silencing Demonic Prediction & Projection*
68) *Silencing Your Mocker*
69) *Understanding the Power of the Holy Ghost*
70) *Understanding the Baptism of Power*
71) *The Mystery of the Blood of Jesus*
72) *Understanding the Mystery of Sanctification*
73) *Understanding the Power of Holiness*
74) *Understanding the Forces of Purity & Righteousness*
75) *Activating the Forces of Vengeance*
76) *Appreciating the Mystery of Restoration*
77) *Overcoming the Projection & Prediction of the Enemy*
78) *Engaging the Mystery of the Blood*
79) *Commanding the Power of the Speaking Faith*
80) *Uprooting the Forces Against Your Rising*
81) *Overcoming Mere Success Syndrome*
82) *Understanding Divine Sentence*
83) *Understanding the Mystery of Praise*
84) *Understanding the Author of Faith*
85) *The Mystery of the Finisher of Faith*
86) *Attracting Supernatural Favor*

MIRACLE OF GOD MINISTRIES

NIGERIA CRUSADE 2012

MIRACLE OF GOD MINISTRIES
NIGERIA CRUSADE
2012

MIRACLE OF GOD MINISTRIES
NIGERIA CRUSADE 2012

MIRACLE OF GOD MINISTRIES

NIGERIA CRUSADE

2012

MIRACLE OF GOD MINISTRIES

NIGERIA CRUSADE

2012

www.ingramcontent.com/pod-product-compliance
Lightning Source LLC
Chambersburg PA
CBHW021450080526
44588CB00009B/774